ART THERAPY COLORING

COLORING BOOKS
FOR TEENS
RELAXATION

Nature Designs

Preview of Coloring Pages

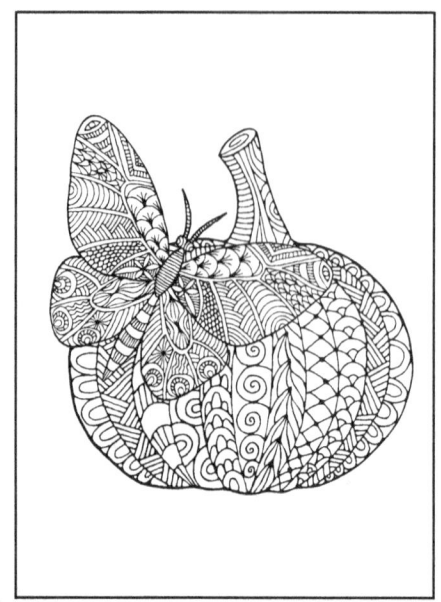

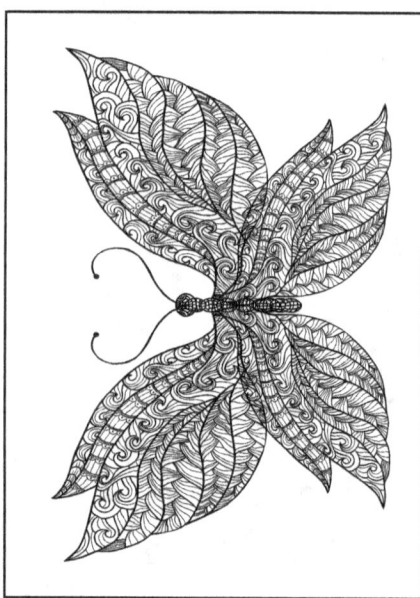

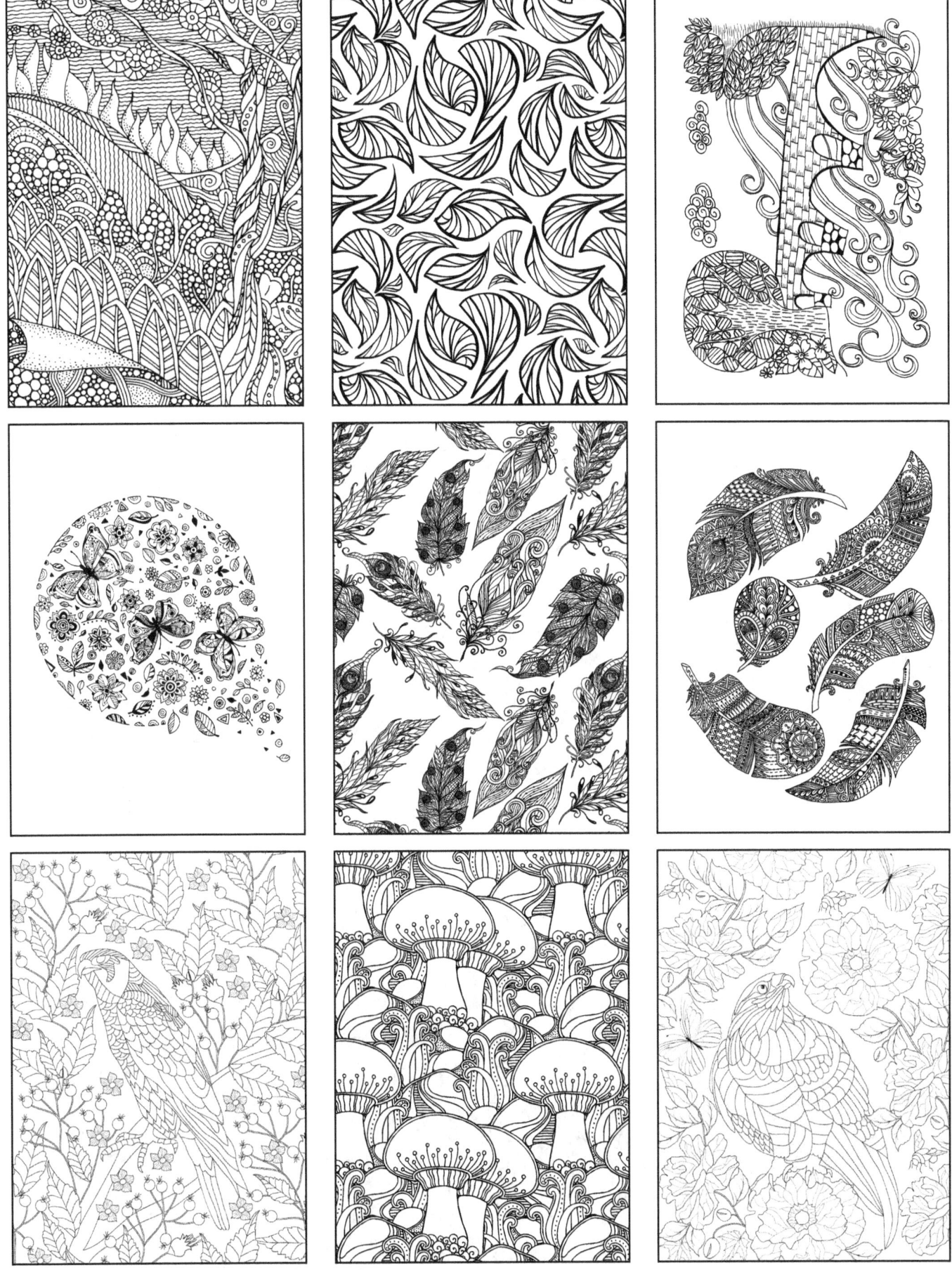

Preview of Coloring Pages

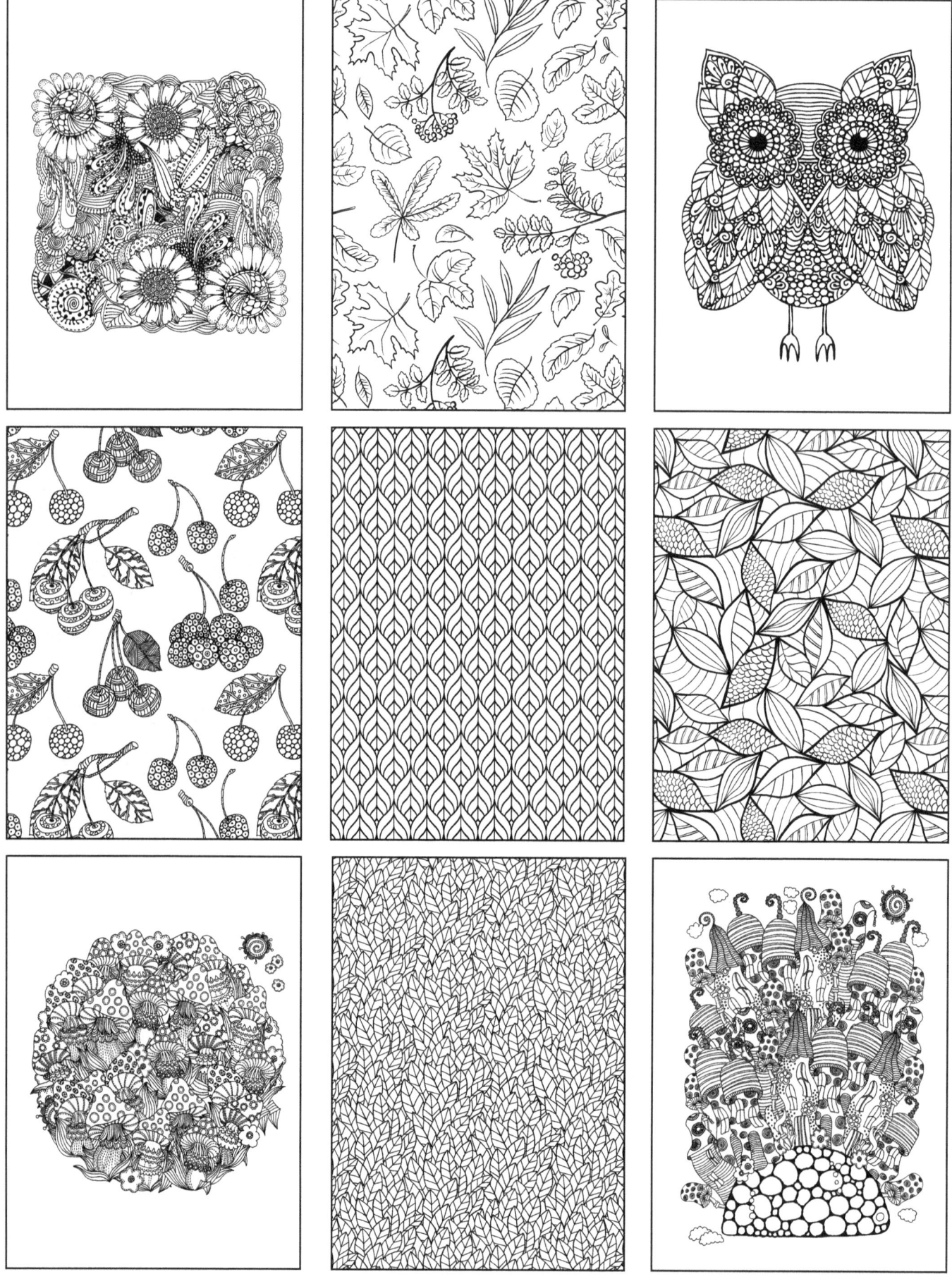

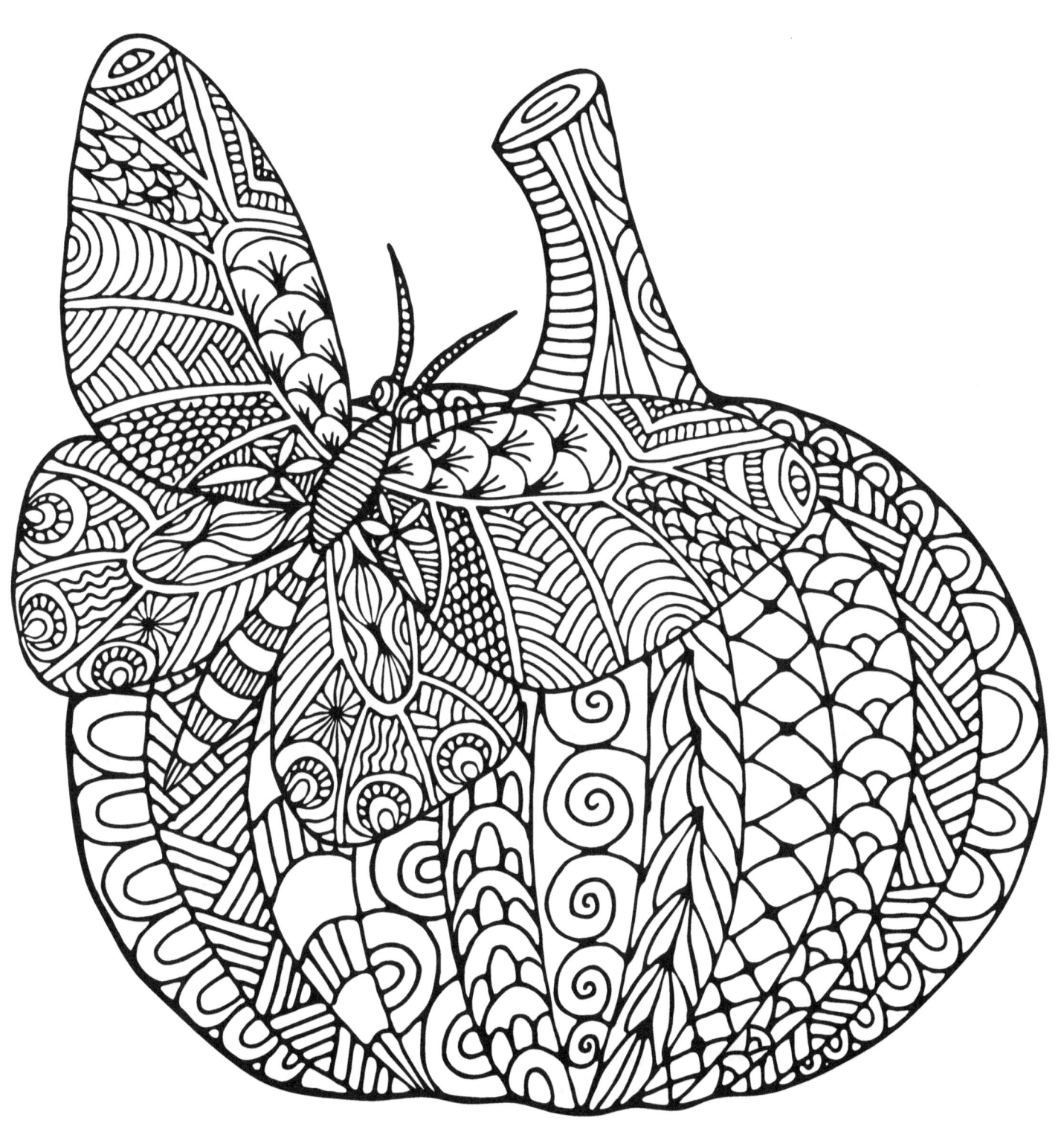

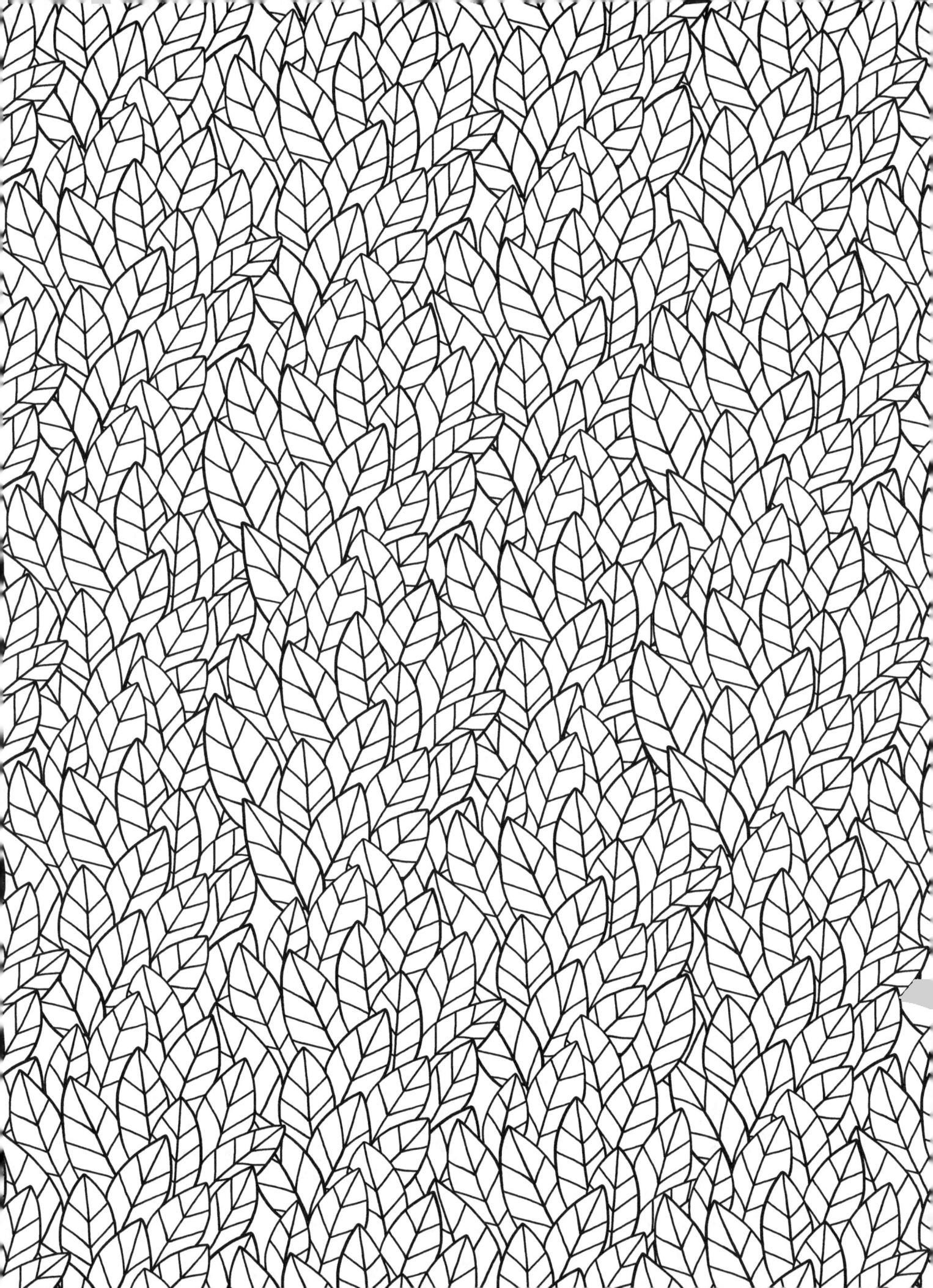

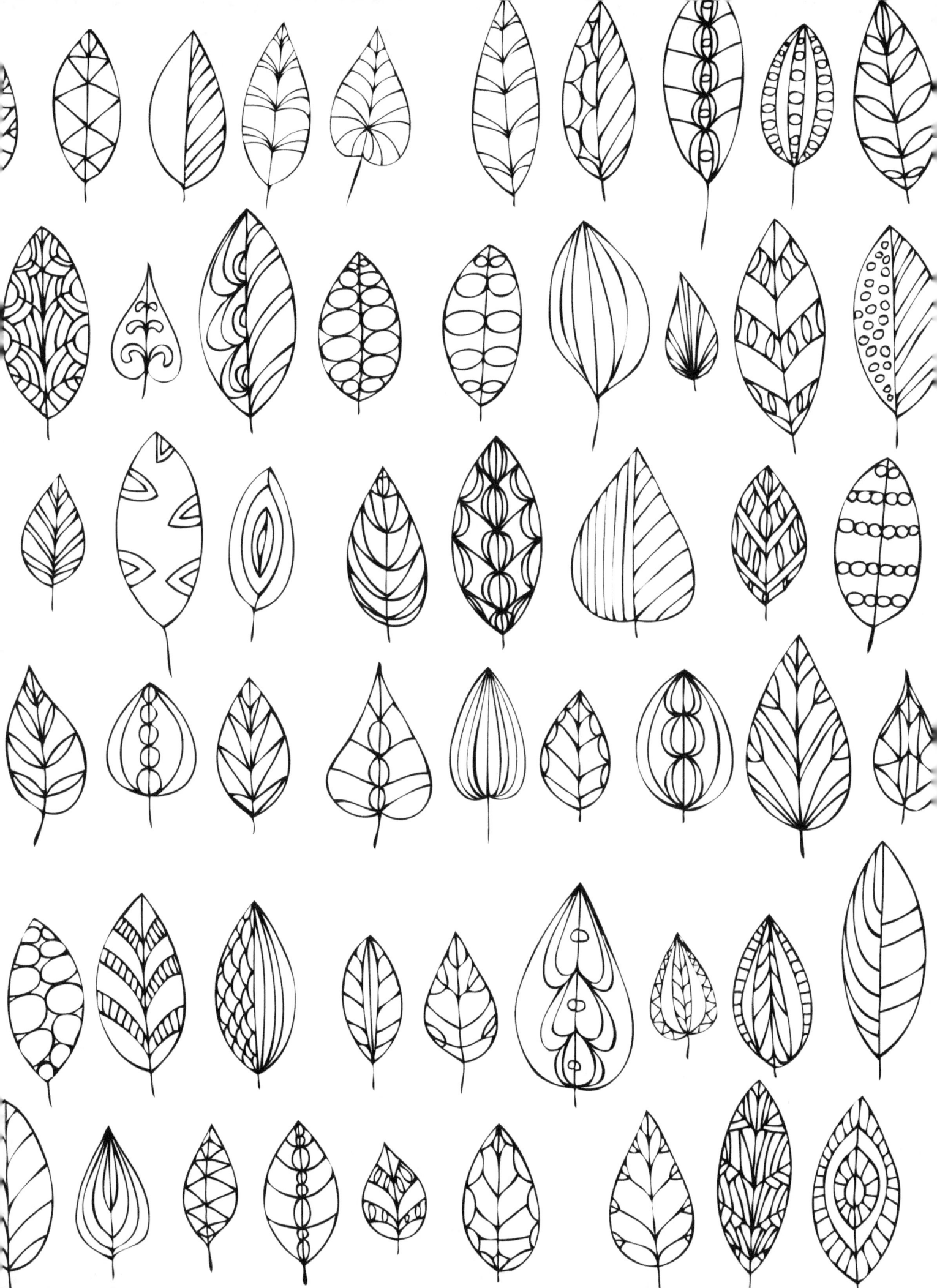

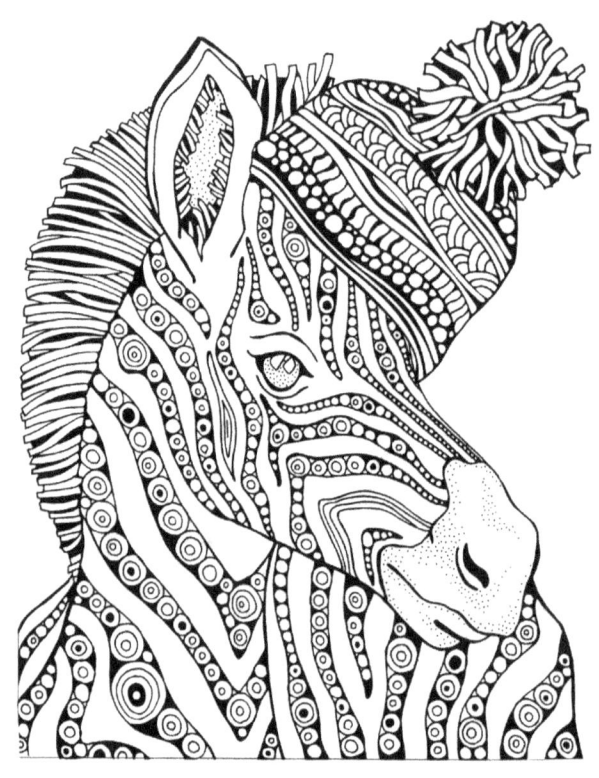

Did You Enjoy Our Coloring Book?

We Want To Hear About It!

Help spread the word about our coloring books! The best way to spread the word is through reviews. We know how busy you are, especially with all of that coloring, but we would appreciate it!

Visit our website at www.arttherapycoloring.com

Over 200 Art Therapy Coloring Books

See our collection of over 200 Art Therapy Coloring Books for Adults, Men, Women, Seniors, Teens, Kids, Boys, and Girls.

Coloring Books For Girls

Art Therapy Coloring Books

COLORING BOOKS FOR TEEN GIRLS DETAILED DESIGNS
Black Background

TEEN GIRLS COLORING BOOKS DETAILED DESIGNS
Native American Inspired

COLORING BOOKS FOR TEENS RELAXATION
Nature Designs

BUTTERFLY COLORING BOOK FOR TEENS

COLORING BOOKS FOR TEEN GIRLS VOL 2 DETAILED DESIGNS

ADULT COLORING BOOKS FOR GIRLS
Detailed Designs

COLORING BOOKS FOR GIRLS DETAILED DESIGNS VOL 1

COLORING BOOKS FOR GIRLS OCEAN DESIGNS

COLORING BOOKS FOR GIRLS RELAXATION
Black Background

COLORING BOOKS FOR OLDER KIDS GEOMETRIC DESIGNS

HEART COLORING BOOK FOR KIDS

DETAILED COLORING BOOKS FOR KIDS
Ocean Designs

ANIMAL COLORING BOOK FOR OLDER KIDS

COLORING BOOKS FOR OLDER KIDS ANIMAL DESIGNS

COLORING BOOKS FOR GIRLS RELAXATION
Butterflies

BUTTERFLY COLORING BOOK FOR KIDS
Detailed Designs

Coloring Books For Kids

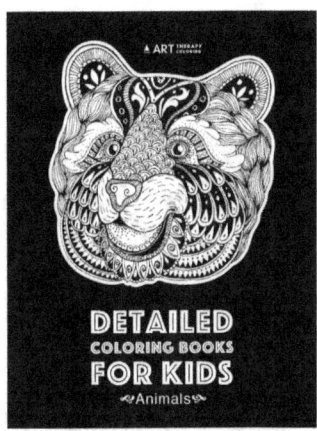

Coloring Books For Boys

COLORING BOOKS **FOR BOYS** WILD ANIMALS
ART THERAPY COLORING

COLORING BOOKS **FOR BOYS** ~DRAGONS~
ART THERAPY COLORING

COLORING BOOKS **FOR BOYS** ANIMAL DESIGNS
ART THERAPY COLORING

COLORING BOOKS **FOR BOYS** OCEAN DESIGNS
Black Background

COLORING BOOKS **FOR BOYS** ~SHARKS~
ART THERAPY COLORING

DINOSAUR COLORING BOOKS **FOR BOYS**
Detailed Designs

COLORING BOOKS **FOR BOYS** NATIVE AMERICAN INSPIRED
ART THERAPY COLORING

COLORING BOOKS FOR BOYS **ANIMALS**
ART THERAPY COLORING

TEEN BOYS COLORING BOOK ANIMAL DESIGNS
ART THERAPY COLORING

TEEN COLORING BOOKS ~ **FOR BOYS** ~ DETAILED DESIGNS
ART THERAPY COLORING

TEEN COLORING BOOKS ~ **FOR BOYS** ~ DETAILED DESIGNS
Black Background

COLORING BOOKS **FOR TEEN BOYS** DETAILED DESIGNS
ART THERAPY COLORING

COLORING BOOKS **FOR TEEN BOYS** DETAILED DESIGNS
Black Background

ADULT COLORING BOOKS **FOR KIDS**
Geometric Designs

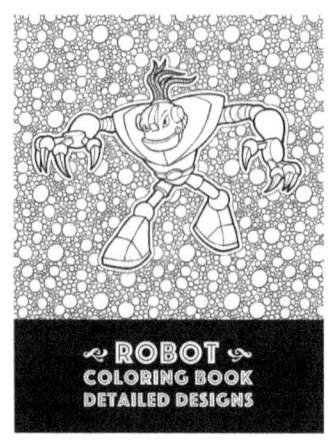

~ **ROBOT** ~ COLORING BOOK DETAILED DESIGNS

DETAILED COLORING BOOKS **FOR KIDS**
Geometric Designs

Coloring Books For Teens

COLORING BOOKS
FOR TEENS
WOLVES & MORE

TEEN
COLORING BOOKS
ANIMAL DESIGNS

TEEN
COLORING BOOKS
ANIMALS
Black Background

COLORING BOOKS
FOR TEENS
OWLS

TEEN
INSPIRATIONAL
COLORING BOOKS

TEEN
COLORING BOOKS
ANIMAL DESIGNS
Black Background

DETAILED
COLORING BOOK
FOR TEENAGERS
Animal Designs

TEEN
COLORING BOOK
INSPIRATIONAL QUOTES

TWEEN COLORING
BOOKS FOR GIRLS
CUTE ANIMALS

ADULT COLORING BOOKS
FOR TEENS
Animal Designs

COLORING BOOKS
FOR TEENS
CAT & DOG DESIGNS

MANDALA
COLORING BOOK
FOR TEENS
Black Background

COLORING BOOKS
FOR TEENS
SEAHORSES & MORE

COLORING BOOKS
FOR TEENS
RELAXATION
Dolphins & More

TEENS
COLORING BOOK
OCEAN THEME

COLORING BOOKS
FOR TEENS
SHARKS & MORE

Coloring Books For Teens

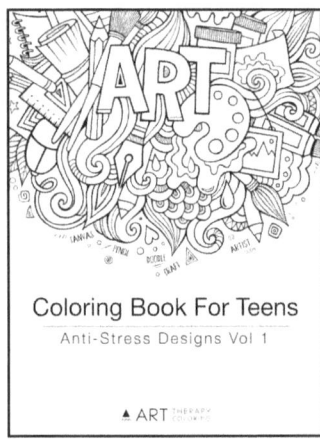

Coloring Book For Teens

Anti-Stress Designs Vol 1

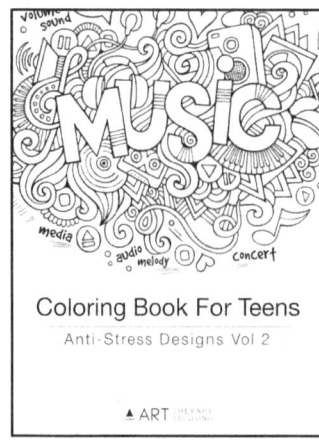

Coloring Book For Teens

Anti-Stress Designs Vol 2

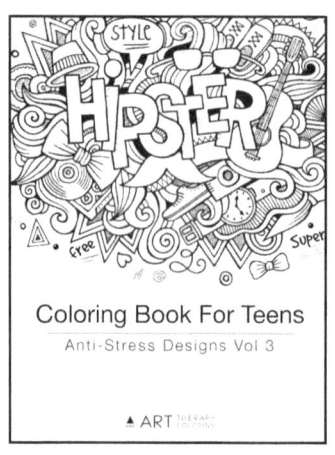

Coloring Book For Teens

Anti-Stress Designs Vol 3

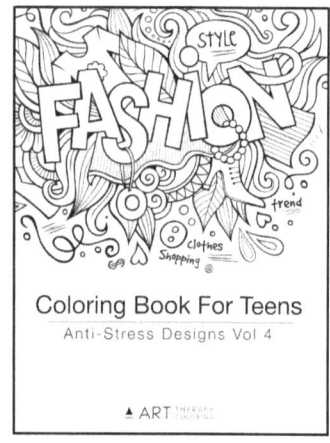

Coloring Book For Teens

Anti-Stress Designs Vol 4

Coloring Book For Teens

Anti-Stress Designs Vol 5

Coloring Book For Teens

Anti-Stress Designs Vol 6

Coloring Book For Teens

Anti-Stress Designs Vol 7

Coloring Book For Teens

Anti-Stress Designs Vol 8

GEOMETRIC COLORING BOOK FOR TEENS

ANIMAL COLORING BOOK FOR TEENS VOL 1

ANIMAL COLORING BOOK FOR TEENS VOL 2

MOTORCYCLE COLORING BOOK FOR TEENS

Black Background

COLORING BOOKS FOR TEENS OCEAN DESIGNS

MERMAID COLORING BOOK FOR TEENS

Black Background

SKULL COLORING BOOK FOR TEENS

Black Background

DINOSAUR COLORING BOOK FOR TEENS

Black Background

Coloring Books For Adults

Coloring Books For Adults

Coloring Books For Adults

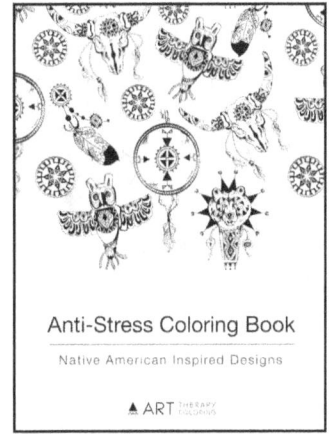

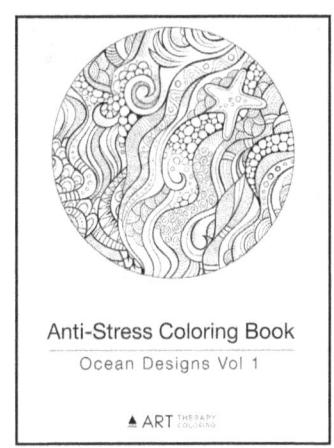

Coloring Books For Seniors

Coloring Book For Seniors
Anti-Stress Designs Vol 1

Coloring Book For Seniors
Nature Designs Vol 1

BUTTERFLY
COLORING BOOK
FOR SENIORS
Black Background

COLORING BOOKS
FOR SENIORS
ANIMAL DESIGNS

MANDALA
COLORING BOOK
FOR SENIORS

MANDALA
COLORING BOOK
FOR SENIORS
Black Background

COLORING BOOKS
FOR SENIORS
HEART DESIGNS

HAPPY BIRTHDAY
TO YOU ON YOUR
70TH BIRTHDAY
Black Background

COLORING BOOKS
FOR SENIORS
SWIRL DESIGNS
Black Background

COLORING BOOKS
FOR SENIORS
RELAXING DESIGNS

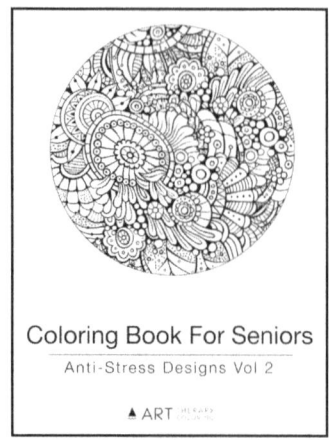

Coloring Book For Seniors
Anti-Stress Designs Vol 2

Coloring Book For Seniors
Anti-Stress Designs Vol 3

Coloring Book For Seniors
Anti-Stress Designs Vol 4

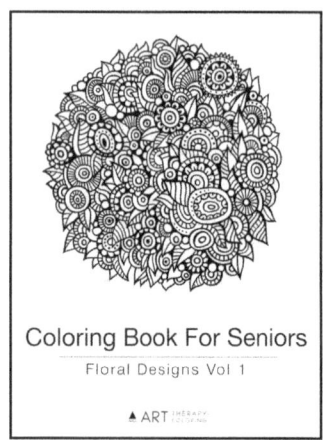

Coloring Book For Seniors
Floral Designs Vol 1

Coloring Book For Seniors
Floral Designs Vol 2

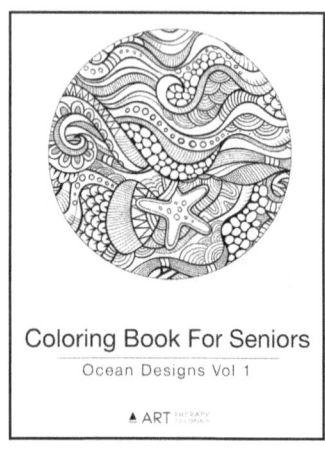

Coloring Book For Seniors
Ocean Designs Vol 1

Coloring Books For Men

Coloring Book For Men
Anti-Stress Designs Vol 1
ART THERAPY COLORING

COLORING BOOK
FOR MEN
ANIMAL DESIGNS
ART THERAPY COLORING

COLORING BOOKS
FOR MEN
HUNTING
ART THERAPY COLORING

Go Fishing
COLORING BOOK
FOR MEN
FISHING DESIGNS

CHOPPER
COLORING BOOK
FOR MEN
BIKER DESIGNS

COLORING BOOK
FOR MEN
SKULL DESIGNS
Black Background

COLORING BOOK
FOR MEN
TATTOO DESIGNS
Black Background

ADULT
COLORING BOOK FOR MEN
ANIMAL DESIGNS
Black Background
ART THERAPY COLORING

ANIMAL
COLORING BOOK
FOR SENIORS MEN

NATURE
COLORING BOOK
FOR SENIORS MEN

OCEAN
COLORING BOOK
FOR SENIORS MEN

COLORING BOOK
FOR MEN
HAPPY BIRTHDAY
Black Background

Coloring Books For Special Occasions

Coloring Books For Teens Relaxation
Nature Designs

Published by:
Art Therapy Coloring
El Dorado Hills, California
www.arttherapycoloring.com

Shutterstock Images

ISBN: 978-1548487898